Rewire Your Brain
And Earn MORE

Destiny S. Harris

...

1st Free Gift!

Giving Rocks.

I give away free books daily. Get your free books today. Here's how

Step 1: Visit amazon.com/author/destinyharris

Step 2: Filter books by "Price: Low to High"

Step 3: Download available free eBooks

...

Table of Contents

Introduction 9

Chapter 1: Old Belief Systems 20

Chapter 2: The Destination 30

Chapter 3: Acquisition Of Knowledge 51

Chapter 4: New Belief Systems 72

Chapter 5: Action 88

Final Thoughts 109

Application 114

Thank You For Reading 121

Leave A Review 122

The End. 123

About Destiny S. Harris 126

Connect W/ Destiny S. Harris 128

Free Gifts! 129

My Recommended Finance Books 130

...

Rewire Your Brain

And Earn MORE

Introduction

I didn't come from wealth, and my parents grew up impoverished.

However, there are two invaluable gifts they gave me.

I received one from each parent.

Gift 1: Exposure

My father gave me the gift of exposure.

He worked with and for a lot of wealthy clients. I tagged along with him whenever the opportunity presented itself.

I had never seen homes or lifestyles such as these people.

One of the people he knew was **Bernie Sanders**.

He and his wife cut me a check to study abroad in China, for which I will forever be grateful.

My father regularly exposed me to these types of people: business owners, venture capitalists, financiers, millionaires, billionaires, owners, entrepreneurs, high-class attorneys, doctors, and the like.

Because of all the jobs I did with him, I was exposed to insane levels of wealth owned by the people he worked with.

Never in my life had I seen homes and interior designs and lives such as these people had. I also noticed how easy it was for them to cut checks for our work.

Sometimes, we would work 1-2 hours and get checks for $500-$1,000. My favorite jobs were the ones where we got the most money for the least amount of work.

Since many people were generous, many often padded the checks with extra green.

This was good and bad; getting paid this much for such little time f*cked my mindset, so I always struggled working regular minimum-wage jobs.

Though I worked in the fast food and retail industries, I couldn't stay long because I always thought back to the work my father exposed me to.

How could I go from earning hundreds or a thousand bucks an hour to earning $7.25 an hour?

Thankfully, my parents encouraged me to start my own music teaching business, which I ran for about ten years.

Though I didn't earn hundreds per hour, I still earned anywhere from $40 to $60 per hour (in middle and high school), which was significantly better than minimum wage, and the money was more consistent than the jobs with my father.

Gift 2: Education

My mother gave me the gift of education. She would pay me to read personal development books.

I read through them so fast that she closed up shop.

But I never stopped reading...

She instilled in me a tenacious animalistic hunger and desire for learning.

Today, I read almost daily; I try not to go a day without reading something.

My parents would have us read Robert T. Kiyosaki books at the dinner table, along with other personal finance books.

At the time, I didn't know what the heck the authors were talking about. But what I did know is I was a consistent piggy bank user; I got a bank account under my mother in elementary school; I started investing when I was 14; I paid my first bill in elementary school; I found ways to fund the many of the things I wanted to do (like travel and study abroad in Europe and Asia, which collectively cost $30,000); and family members always came to me for loans.

Something in the books was clicking for me subconsciously because I always had money or was figuring out ways to obtain it.

Early on, being broke would never be an option for me. I would always have and be someone who could help and give to others.

Why I'm Writing This Series

I've considered writing this series for the last couple of months. I finally sat the f*ck down and started writing it because something in my mind kept telling me to do it.

This information needs to get out and be shared amongst our community.

The more knowledge we have, the more we increase our chance of elevating and transforming our financial situations.

*I would not be where I am today without **books**; it's the primary way I obtain knowledge.*

Not only does my wealth increase daily, but it increases yearly. There is no such thing as lack; abundance is the only variable that exists.

If you are reading this book, congratulations.

You have taken a step to shift your mindset to foster the right mind to attract and create money into your existence.

Finish the book.

I guarantee there will be at least one takeaway you can share with someone else and apply to your life.

Why Is "Rewiring Your Brain" The Starting Point?

I chose "Rewire Your Brain" as the first book of the series because, without the right mindset, you will never become wealthy.

I've often had to kick myself because old belief systems limited my earning potential. The more limiting belief systems you have, the less success you will experience.

Still, ultimately, my mindset has always been skewed towards wealth, which is why I continue to attract it into my existence, which is precisely what you will also do.

Cheers.

...

...

Chapter 1: Old Belief Systems

The average person has several old belief systems surrounding money that keep them in the same financial position.

Many are unaware of their thoughts about money because they've had them throughout their lives.

Furthermore, the people they acquired these belief systems from were likely their family and friends.

When you come from a wealthy family, you think about money differently than a family from poverty or living paycheck to paycheck.

Most people land financially around the middle or lower class, which means they likely have a lack mentality about money.

Old Belief Systems

1. I can't afford that.

2. That's out of my budget.

3. Money doesn't grow on trees.

4. I wish I could buy that.

5. I wish I could live like that.

6. That's expensive.

7. That's too expensive.

8. I never have enough to do the things I desire.

9. The rich have everything.

10. My income is set.

11. I could never earn six figures.

12. I could never earn millions of dollars.

13. That's out of my range.

14. Maybe in the future.

15. Eventually, I'll be able to engage in an experience like that.

16. I hope to start traveling eventually.

17. One day, I'll (fill in the blank).

18. I'll never be financially independent or free.

19. I'm broke.

20. Earning money is hard.

...

Chapter Summary

Many of us have limiting beliefs, and many of these limiting beliefs were inherited from family and friends throughout our lives.

If you carry limiting beliefs, you will prevent the flow of money, success, and favor into your life.

Think about the limiting beliefs most prominent in your life and replace them with a new belief.

<u>Example</u>

Limiting Belief:

I always have more month than money at the end of every month.

New Belief:

I always have more than enough money to pay

for my expenses and luxuries.

Affirmation: Abundance is my experience.

What limiting belief systems do you have about money? Write them down here, or take a minute to think about them.

____

____

____

____

____

____

____

____

____

____

____

____

...

...

Chapter 2: The Destination

Where do you want to be in one year, three years, five years, ten years, and twenty years?

I always think back to an exercise I completed as a little girl; I wrote down many things I wanted to be when I turned 30. This was an excellent goal exercise.

But more importantly, my mother had my siblings, and I write down our goals every year when we were kids.

Every December or around New Year's Eve, we would write down our goals for the upcoming year.

I no longer practice end-year goal writing. Creating, reviewing, and refining your goals daily, weekly, monthly, or quarterly is more effective. You should be constantly reviewing your goals, though.

Today, I spent about an hour reworking my goals. I cut out all the superfluous goals to increase my focus.

Now, I've gained about 10x more clarity.

You have to know (with 100% clarity) where you're going.

The Destination

If you don't know your intended destination, you will drift.

A powerful book I've read (that I'm going to read again) is called, "Outwitting The Devil."

Don't let the title deceive you; it's not about religion but about how 99% of people are drifters who allow life to push them this way and that.

They succumb to mediocrity via their habits, thoughts, and actions.

When an NFL team plays their opponent, what is their goal?

Well, they have two goals:

1. Win
2. Play their absolute best; it's all or nothing.

The only way to win is by avoiding taking convenient paths through life. You have to give it your all. You can't let fear paralyze you from acting towards your desired destination.

Here's an example.

Let's say you're earning $50,000 a year. This is a decent salary, but you could earn significantly more, just like Kim Kardashian earns billions to simply be herself.

It doesn't take significant skill or talent to make money in this day and age.

All it takes is desire and the will to experience your definition of financial success.

The average person earning $50,000 will continue earning this amount because they won't change their actions. Here are some alternate paths you could take to increase your income:

1. Apply for a new job until they get one.

2. Add an income source leveraging a skill.

3. Move around in their current company to a higher-paying position.

4. Seek a raise.

5. Put their money to work by investing.

6. Start educating themselves on how to earn
more money.

But your average person will accept the $50,000,
hoping they get a 3% raise or lightning strikes
and hands them an opportunity.

STOP WAITING FOR OPPORTUNITY.
CREATE OPPORTUNITY. MAKE
SOMETHING OUT OF NOTHING.

Even though my family had no wealth, I refused
to be poor, broke, and economically
disadvantaged.

As a kid, I made sure always to have money. I
was never without. When I was close to running
out, I was on the hunt for more.

I was the loaner, not the loanee.

And I knew my destination would always be financial independence because it was what I set out to accomplish.

I committed early on that I would live differently than many people who surrounded me throughout my life.

"Struggling" would never be in my cards.

The first time I set out to get my first corporate job, I would wake up at 4 a.m., workout at 5 a.m., start applying and interview at 6:30 a.m., and work until 6 or 8 p.m.

You couldn't distract me for nothing. I was so locked in you might've thought I'd gone mad.

For three months straight, this was my routine. I didn't have friends. I didn't check in with people.

I was ruthless about my goals, which is why I finally landed a role that jumpstarted my tech career.

You have a higher chance of landing in the right place when you have an intended destination.

It wasn't convenient to wake up that early.

It wasn't convenient to apply for thousands of jobs.

It wasn't convenient to get rejection emails.

It wasn't convenient to live a highly disciplined lifestyle.

It wasn't convenient to make sacrifices.

But when two offers fell into my lap, all of the inconvenience, effort, and letdowns paid off.

I kept my eyes on my destination to improve my financial outcomes.

Mindset

Mindset is critical.

If your mindset is incorrect, you will set your mind on the wrong destinations.

Some of you may be dreaming too small.

Some of you may be dreaming someone else's dreams.

Some of you may be barely dreaming.

Some of you may dream too big because you believe that will bring you happiness.

Success and money won't make you happy; though they can add happiness to your life, happiness is internally driven. It has to come from you and you alone.

What is your mindset?

Where are you headed?

If you were to maintain your current habits, where would you be in one year, three years, five years, or ten years?

Are you happy with the destinations you envision?

If not, change your habits IMMEDIATELY.

Distractions

We all face distractions. For some of you, it's relationships, dating, social media, television, kids, eating, shopping, hanging out with friends, unexpected pregnancies, gaming, the internet,

YouTube videos, or doing low-value tasks instead of high-value and challenging tasks.

What's your biggest distraction?

After moving into a new place, I decided I wouldn't own any televisions for a while. I still have an iPad, which I use sometimes, but I rarely watch TV when locked in on a goal.

My mindset is different when I'm locked in. In my free time, I'm not looking to waste it on television; instead, I want to get some extra sleep because I'm **WORKING**.

Ya, feel me?

Distractions are fun. They're easy to engage in.

They're easy to give your hours, days, and weeks to. It's another reason I keep my phone silent or in do-not-disturb mode.

But I took it a step further; sometimes, I don't check messaging apps for days or even a week at a time.

The only people who understand this level of detachment from the world are people who also have sh*t going on in their lives.

The rest of the people keep asking where I'm at and why I disappear so frequently.

When you're not distracted, you will lose friends.

But your real friends (and family) will be there for you when you return.

You might even lose partners or dates. It always intrigues me how some non-ambitious people get upset with ambitious people. I always laugh and keep it moving.

*Avoid surrounding yourself with people who ain't sh*t, aren't doing sh*t, and don't have sh*t to lose.*

It's convenient to get caught up with distractions.

It's painful to say **NO** to distractions, which is why most people give in; they don't know how to say NO to themselves because they don't can't see the long-term benefit, and they don't have boundaries.

Most people focus on short-term pleasure instead of long-term outcomes.

We allow people to push past our boundaries often because we push past our own boundaries.

When you don't love yourself, you don't respect your time and dreams. Hence, other people don't respect your time and your dreams.

One of my favorite sayings is, **"Pain Is Good."**

It's a reminder never to give in to what is easy.

The most inconvenient and challenging tasks are the most rewarding.

...

Chapter Summary

<u>The Destination</u>

The question of the day is, where are you headed?

Some of you are headed on the road to nowhere (aka mediocrity), as many people are.

Some of you continue taking detours because you're getting distracted by whatever life throws your way.

Some of you haven't clarified your goals well enough.

Until you define your destination (the goal), you will wander.

Clearly define your destination.

Mindset

The right mindset is focused, determined, tenacious, and locked in.

Without the proper mindset, you will waver on your journey to your destination.

Commit once, or don't commit at all.

To transform your financial situation, you must foster the right mindset, and the right mindset is dangerous.

As soon as you pivot into the right mindset, doors open wide open for you, or you're busting through them and creating the opportunities you seek.

Distractions

Distractions will eat you alive.

Learn to implement boundaries with yourself, your time, and your goals.

As you become more locked into your dreams, be prepared to lose people.

Not everyone will be happy with your limited availability. But the right people will never take issue with it.

Focus on long-term outcomes over short-term pleasure.

Affirmation: I am locked in and focused on reaching my intended destination.

What is my goal destination? Where am I headed based on my current habits? Am I happy with where I'm heading?

...

...

Chapter 3: Acquisition Of Knowledge

Back To Childhood Gifts

I'll always be grateful to my parents for that library of books they had in the house.

But they did more than that.

We all went to the library together all the time; I still read and check out books from the library.

My mother would also make my siblings and I read daily. She would set the timer for 30 minutes and were stuck with books until the bell rang.

But the truth is, I enjoyed it, and so did my siblings. I recall reading several books to my sister growing up. And my brother blasted through books faster than humanly possible.

I genuinely love reading. I tend to approach reading with a ferocious spirit.

I recently listened to Ann Marie Smith, who highlighted that she reads about 3-4 books a week. I was inspired.

Since my schedule is off the rails sometimes, I don't always take the time to sit down and finish a paperback in one sitting.

So, I took up audiobooks again, as I used to on my 3-hour commutes living in the northeast.

I'm back to completing 3 to 5 (or more) books a week, and it feels f*cking amazing because I'm growing at an elevated and rapid pace.

Here's the thing:

The more you learn, the more you earn.

Every time I complete a book, I earn more, or an idea or person comes into my life that helps me earn more.

The acquisition of knowledge is one of the most underestimated resources that, too frequently, people don't take advantage of.

Free Resources Are As Valuable As Paid Ones

Many resources are thankfully **free.**

I only read certain books more than once; many others are one-and-done. Consequently, I aim to read books from the library, online PDFs, or borrow from friends and family.

Not only does it save money, but it prevents waste and aligns with my minimalistic values.

Don't get me wrong, I still invest my money.

There are courses and books I still buy, but If I can acquire knowledge for free, why wouldn't I?

Even this book I offer for free several days a year so that people can access the knowledge for no cost. And that goes with many of my books.

Every single day, I'm giving away books for free.

Too much information is out there available to those who are willing to learn. And there is no point in hoarding knowledge.

If you have an abundance mindset, your actions will be skewed towards giving.

Many will say you don't value the information as much if you don't pay for a resource.

I beg to differ.

Most books and content I read, watch, or listen to are free. Yet, I consume the content with an animalistic attitude. I take nothing for granted.

If anything, I'm even more grateful I raised my awareness, earnings, and knowledge for FREE.

I usually recommend books in my articles and other books or everyday conversations with people to help promote it and spread the word.

It's all about your attitude.

People say you must attend thousand-dollar seminars or get a fancy mentor to succeed.

Once again, I disagree.

You're in a strong position if you're reading books, watching seminars online, listening to podcasts, surrounding yourself with elevating relationships, and committing to learning.

And if you're consuming valuable content daily or reading several books a week, you will be a different person because you're evolving rapidly.

It's not about what you pay but what you apply.

If one person pays for resources and the other doesn't, it doesn't matter if both people *don't* apply the knowledge they just learned.

They will both be in the same position, except one person is poorer since they spent money.

Become Addicted To Acquiring Knowledge

I started a book club, thinking no one would be interested, but several people joined.

But too few still read.

90% of people buy televisions. 10% buy business books (Robert T. Kiyosaki).

My goal is to help others learn invaluable concepts to better themselves.

To me, reading is more fun than going out because I know that knowledge will empower me to experience a better life.

For some of you, reading books could help you create a life so that you can always go out and have fun instead of only on the weekends.

The people who learn the most (and apply) are the ones who stay ahead of the ball game.

If you're reading this book, this is a telling sign, that you're willing to put in the effort to shift your financial and life outcomes.

But you can't stop here. You have to continue. It might be this book that helps you or the 100th book down the road that provides you with the information you need.

You can't stop learning even after that 100th book, though, or you will stifle your progress.

I became addicted to learning as a kid.

Occasionally, I experience bouts where I don't **feel** like learning, which usually means my teachability index is low. It is usually because I've learned so much information and need a breather.

But once I'm ready, I return to that classroom and continue learning.

Never Take A Day Off

I'm trying to recall which book mentioned this idea, but the premise suggested that the elite never take days off from learning -- even when they're vacationing.

Ordinary people use vacation to stop working out, eat like slobs, and not do anything productive with their minds.

It's okay to vacation, take breaks and splurge, but the one thing you should never cease exercising is your mind.

Commit to reading one sentence, section, or page daily of something that will elevate your mind.

Commit to excellence.

How To Improve Your Financial Situation

If you don't come from or understand money, you must invest time, energy, and effort into learning about money.

Furthermore, you must break out of your old mentality and limiting beliefs about money. The only way to do this is through education.

Every month, I'm intaking personal finance books, and with the powerful reading method of audiobooks, there are some months I could end up reading multiple finance books.

The key here is I never stop learning. The more I learn, the more I earn.

Black women typically don't come from wealth; moreover, we're usually not taught about money.

I had to learn about money with my parents at the dinner table. They were learning with me.

However, my real financial education didn't start until I began reading personal finance books on my own to understand and thoroughly digest the concepts.

I had to re-read "Rich Dad, Poor Dad" several times before it clicked, and it's a SIMPLE BOOK.

Finance and economics are such vast subjects.

We don't have to be experts; we just need the proper knowledge to help us reach our goals and shift our financial outcomes into ones we want.

I didn't learn the game of investing (which I'm still learning) solely by reading; I had to execute.

Learn and apply.

The only way I become a more skilled investor is through application and practice in the real world.

The same goes for increasing my income. I can't just read about how to increase my income; I must put ideas into motion to learn what works and doesn't.

You must do the same.

...

Chapter Summary

<u>Back To Childhood Gifts</u>

My parents had a library in their home with many influential books.

We read books at the dinner table, they took us to the library (which I still go to today), and they made us read for at least 30 minutes a day until the bell rang.

All of these gifts brought me to where I am today.

Books are powerful. Books are magical. We become different people after each book we read.

<u>Free Resources Are As Valuable As Paid Ones</u>

Much of the content I consume is free, but it doesn't make it any less valuable. Start with books if you're uncomfortable spending hundreds or thousands of dollars on a course, seminar, or other learning opportunities.

They've been the primary reason I've gotten to where I am today.

If books can work for me, I know they can also work for you.

Become Addicted To Acquiring Knowledge

The most successful people are some of the most ardent readers.

Warren Buffet reads hours daily, and it seems to work insatiably well for him since he's one of the wealthiest people in the world.

Never stop learning.

Continue expanding your circle with intelligent, wholesome, and evolving people.

Never Take A Day Off

Practice the daily acquisition of knowledge.

Never go a day without learning -- even when you're vacationing.

Most people don't fast and take days off from eating.

Apply the same logic to your mind.

Feed your mind daily.

How To Improve Your Financial Situation

The easiest way to improve your financial situation is via self-education.

Invest your time, effort, and energy into learning, then practice applying the information.

You can't stay in simulation mode forever; you must execute to practice what you've learned in the real world.

Affirmation: I am addicted to learning and applying insightful knowledge.

What is the last book I read outside of this one?

What is the next book I'm going to read?

...

...

Chapter 4: New Belief Systems

I've never said, "I'm broke" or "I don't have any money."

And interestingly enough, most people don't know me to be a broke person.

Even if I didn't have the money I desired, I always acted as if I had because that's who I always saw myself to be.

Instead of focusing on lack, I focus on abundance.

Instead of focusing on financial worry, I focus on having more than enough.

But I still struggled with my belief systems. Most of my struggle came down to waiting and procrastination.

For years, I didn't travel because I thought I no longer had the desire. I popped that cherry after heading back to Europe after six years and exploring ten countries. Months later, I took a two-month trip to Europe, Asia, and Africa.

Interestingly enough, it was after my visit to Istanbul, Turkey, that everything changed for me.

I busted through the bubble of fear and felt liberated, at peace, and abundant on my travels through the Middle East.

I ended up staying in different parts of the Middle East for weeks and look forward to going back.

What happened?

Why did it take me six years to start traveling internationally again?

It wasn't COVID because my travels stopped before the pandemic.

It was my own internalized fears and self-imposed limitations.

I thought it was too expensive.

I thought I didn't have the time.

I thought it wasn't feasible since I have multiple dogs.

I thought it didn't make sense for my lifestyle since I'm amply physically active.

But these were all dumb excuses I told myself to convince myself the adventurous travel bunny no longer existed as it did back in the day.

My parents took us across the country, Canada, and Mexico, and before I graduated high school, I took my first big girl trip to six European countries.

Traveling has always been one of my favorite things to do.

But I subconsciously thought I couldn't afford it even though I could.

*It's cheaper to travel than people think. What determines the amount you spend is how long you desire to travel and **how** you want to travel.*

The more luxurious you travel, the more the experience may cost.

If you want to travel luxuriously, do it.

Don't let financial barriers restrain you. Just be sure you don't go into debt to make it a reality.

My New Belief System

I travel 3-4 months internationally every year. I usually travel to about ten or more countries at a time, and it's easy for me to do. I believe in maxing it out when I travel -- as it's one of my favorite areas to spend money on, and I don't apologize to anyone for being gone for extended periods.

How did I arrive at this mindset?

It was a few days after my birthday while I was in Rome, Italy, with my sister.

The trip was about to end, and I looked over at my sister and told her, "Let's keep going."

She was down.

Life is short. I didn't feel like going home yet, and we were already there.

Why not make it an even grander trip?

After that, I became used to traveling for 1-2 months at a time.

It feels normal.

Many people are just trying to get in a one-week vacation.

One of my friends told me he's trying to travel like me. I thought to myself, "What's stopping him?"

Of course, he's stopping himself, but we often do this, too.

We think an invisible barrier prevents us from acquiring our desires when, in reality, it's our limited thinking.

Here's what I've learned:

If you want to make something happen, you'll make it happen.

All the stuff you say you want, but you refuse to go after tenaciously, you don't really want it.

Read that sentence again.

The next time you tell yourself you want to experience or attain something, remind yourself that you're lying to yourself if you take no action to manifest it.

<u>Back to my new belief system:</u>

There is no such thing as lack; this is a human-made concept.

There is more than enough for everyone.

Abundance is the only experience in existence **UNLESS** you believe lack is your existence.

We create our realities.

If you believe in lack, you will create lack.

If you believe in abundance, you will create abundance.

...

Chapter Summary

My New Belief System

I never thought I was broke, but I subconsciously thought I was. You could see this from my actions because I was acting broke.

Though I had financial resources, I refused to engage in one of my favorite activities in the world: Travel.

I even thought I didn't want to travel for a time. I was content being and staying in place. My exploration and curiosity bugs were dead.

I stopped engaging in my favorite activity for years because I was afraid and thought I couldn't manage it.

My New Belief System

After breaking through the bubble in Rome, Italy, and Istanbul, Turkey, I now travel 1-2 months internationally at a time.

During one of my trips, my sister watched a movie, and the mother told her daughter, "I wish I would've taken more risks, explored more, traveled the world, and stopped being so damn scared."

Something about those words struck my soul. From there, I told my sister, let's go to Turkey after all (previously hesitation filled my body about visiting).

Then, we visited Dubai, UAE, Oman, Qatar, Egypt, India, and other European countries.

I'm the only person imposing limitations on myself.

You're the only person imposing limitations on yourself.

What is it that you desire most ardently?

Write it down.

Create an execution path and make it your reality.

The only barrier between you and your dream is **you.**

Affirmation: I am creating my ideal universe.

What are my primary desires? What's stopping
me from making them a reality?

...

...

Chapter 5: Action

Procrastination is opportunity's assassin (Victor Kiam).

I'm reading "The Power of One More" by Ed Mylett (a fascinating book I encourage you to read), and the quote above popped up.

It hit me like a ton of bricks because I thought back to all the times I allowed procrastination to get the best of me.

For example, the idea of this book series came into existence months ago. I write daily, but for some reason, I refused to get started on this book because I was "overwhelmed" with other projects.

But the whole time, this project produced the most excitement and desire.

Thankfully, I'm writing the book now, but it could've already been on the market helping women around the globe.

Another example is moving to different states. I lived in the Southwest for four years, knowing good and well I was ready to move to the West Coast.

What prevented me from moving?

Fear and excuses all result in procrastination.

Once I moved to the West Coast, my entire life changed.

I experienced rapid growth, and it seems like I become an entirely new person every month on the West Coast because of how much knowledge I'm being exposed to, how much higher my vibrations are, and the people surrounding me now versus then.

My life is 100 times better, but I kept waiting for the right time to move.

It was always the right time to move, but I kept delaying the opportunity.

Don't wait for the perfect moment. Seize or create the moment you desire.

The funny part is once I finally decided to move, I decided in less than a week and was living in an entirely new state, all within 24 hours thanks to my heroic father, who helped me complete the move with my four dogs.

Sometimes, I wonder what life would have been like if I had moved sooner.

Ultimately, I know I moved when I was ready, but I promised never to procrastinate on anything I genuinely desired again.

Go for it, and make it happen.

When a desire pops up, find a way to make it happen.

When an idea pops up into your mind, experiment with it. You'll only know it doesn't work after you consistently invest effort.

When an opportunity comes knocking, open the door and welcome it in for dinner.

The Peril Of Information

We live in the information age, meaning information is everywhere.

Everything we need to know is right at our fingertips.

We only need to look in the right places.

But if you're not careful, you'll become an information addict that never acts.

Information addicts are some of the most brilliant people on the planet, but many never act.

They know all the strategies and simulations of these strategies, but they never get out on the practice field to try them out.

They get excited whenever they learn new information but never have the clit to execute.

Without execution, you might as well have never learned the information in the first place.

The only way you'll ever experience or create wealth for yourself is through the execution of ideas and knowledge.

Fear is a powerful emotion.

Most people procrastinate because they're afraid to fail; they're afraid of risks; they're afraid to lose.

But winners are winners because they're not afraid to lose.

Once you can get past the fear of losing and taking risks, you'll be unstoppable.

I recall the first time I made a $10,000 investment in a speculative asset. To the world, it was a dumb move.

When the broker asked if I was ready to execute, part of my being screamed, "Tell him to cut it by 50% and drop it $5,000!"

But something within me told me to respond confidently and calmly with, "Yes, let's proceed."

After that transaction, I was different; it was the beginning of bigger investment deals.

If you want to win, you can't be afraid to lose.

If you want to shift your financial outcomes, you can't keep doing the same bullsh*t you've always done.

You got to go big, and you got to go hard.

Most people will remain broke all their lives because they fear risk. Hence, they will never go against the grain.

One of the best pieces of advice I ever came across was:

If you desire success, do the opposite of what most do.

Since I've been exposed to this advice, I aim to live differently than most.

1. I invest in assets more than liabilities.

2. I am a hybrid minimalist because materials can't bring happiness. Having less means having more freedom.

3. I don't live paycheck to paycheck.

4. I focus my efforts on creating passive income.

5. I give generously and consistently.

6. I invest over 50% of my income every month.

7. I actively monitor my financial portfolio instead of leaving it solely in the hands of others.

8. I am uninterested in how people view how I
live because the only person I'm trying to impress
is myself.

Why Are You Driving That Old Thing?

People always wondered why I drove my car for
over a decade when I could have bought a luxury
vehicle.

I knew I would get a luxury vehicle when ready,
but it had to be on my terms.

I wasn't getting it just because I could or to
impress people.

I put several stipulations in place before buying
my next car:

Stipulation 1:
Pay off my car in 3 years instead of 6.

Stipulation 2:

Maintain my car without buying a new one for at least ten years.

Stipulation 3:

Go without a car payment for at least seven years.

Stipulation 4:

Have the cash in the bank to purchase my new car whenever I'm ready. I would never go into debt again to buy a car.

Stipulation 5:

Reach 200k miles. I really wanted to leave my mark on the car, which I kept, by the way.

But once I reached my 200k mile mark, which coincidently happened right when I moved to the West Coast, I was free to get my new car.

Stipulation 6:

Take care of my car like it's a baby. And this always holds true.

Many people think my first car is new, but it's almost two decades old.

You would only know how old my car is by checking out the mileage, which is in the hundreds of thousands.

I always take care of my car -- no matter how old.

If you're not a good steward of what you have, never expect the universe to give you more.

According to PIRG, over 85% of Americans have a car note.

The worst part about this is they have more liabilities than assets, and they're likely planning to upgrade their car as soon as they pay it off or even before they pay it off.

People **love** being in debt, and it's so easy to stay in it throughout life.

Debt Free Or New Car?

A friend of mine had $1,000 left on their car.

Instead of enjoying the overhead decrease, they invested their money in a brand-new $40,000 vehicle.

Their insurance premium was about $200, and the car payment was about $500. They added almost a grand of liabilities to their monthly overhead costs.

What did I do?

Instead of buying a new car like most of my friends were doing, I endured the consistent criticism of people who made jabs at my car --

even though many were broke and continued my efforts of investing and saving -- all to build a robust net worth.

Never take advice from broke people unless you want to be broke.

Chapter Summary

Procrastination is opportunity's assassin (Victor Kiam).

The more we procrastinate, the farther away we will move from manifesting our dreams.

The Peril Of Information

Information is abundant, but if you're not careful, you could become paralyzed by it.

Focus on consuming information, filtering it out, and then acting immediately.

Why Are You Driving That Old Thing?

Many people never understood why I continued to drive the same car year after year -- even though I could afford a better one.

The reason is that I love my car (duh, hello), and I took care of my car; I never hated my car.

I knew that before I got my next car, I had to meet a few stipulations, which included:

.

Stipulation 1:
Pay off my car in 3 years instead of 6.

Stipulation 2:
Maintain my car without buying a new one for at least ten years.

Stipulation 3:
Go without a car payment for at least seven years.

Stipulation 4:
Have the cash in the bank to purchase my new car whenever I'm ready.

Stipulation 5:
Reach 200k miles.

Stipulation 6:

Take care of my car like it's a baby.

My next car purchase would be planned, intentional, and cash-only. Furthermore, my priority was building my net worth (assets), not my liabilities.

Debt Free Or New Car?

A friend chose to buy a new car instead of paying off the $1,000 left on their car note.

Most people choose debt instead of financial freedom, so they live mediocre lives at best.

Never take advice from broke people unless you want to be broke.

Affirmation: I'm addicted to taking action.

Do I act, or do I procrastinate? If I procrastinate, what do I fear?

...

...

Final Thoughts

<u>**Taking Action**</u>

Whenever I finish reading a book, I ask myself what I can apply from what I've learned.

Right before completing "Rich Dad, Poor Dad" by Robert T. Kiyosaki for the fifth time, I made that $10,000 investment.

While reading "You Are A Badass At Making Money" by Jen Sincero, I increased my income by a third and added two new revenue streams.

Books aren't meant for you to read and forget.

Books are here to inspire you to act and become wealthy, more successful, productive, wiser, and happier.

What is one thing you can do now that differs from anything you've done before?

What action can you take today to move you closer to your goals?

Once you identify the answer to this question, act; do not wait under any circumstances.

I don't care how scared, overwhelmed, or cynical you're feeling; get your *ss moving and create change so you can stop experiencing mediocre results.

...

...

Application

What did I learn from this reading:

What will I apply immediately today from this
book?

____

____

____

____

____

____

____

____

____

____

____

____

____

...

...

Thank You For Reading

I appreciate you taking the time to read this book. I speak life, blessings, favor, million-dollar ideas, love, and abundance over your life.

Thank you for reading!

Leave A Review

Feedback is essential to me. Please let me know your takeaways from the book or what information you'd like me to include in the following books.

Thank you for reading!

The End.

...

...

About Destiny S. Harris

Destiny S. Harris' goal is to positively inspire, cultivate, elevate, and educate the minds of individuals across the globe through her writing.

Creating (whether books, courses, articles, poetry, or music) has always been Destiny's thing, not to mention health & fitness and all things entrepreneurial. Destiny published her first book, "Beauty Secrets for Girls," at age 11 and her second book, "Don't Wait Until It's Too Late," at age 12.

Destiny obtained three degrees from the University of Georgia in Psychology, Political Science, & Cultural Studies. She also started her own music teaching business at the age of 14, which she led for over ten years. In addition, she has been teaching academic, career, and personal development topics to thousands of students and readers since 2004.

Outside of writing, Destiny loves and enjoys a few other things: reading, bodybuilding, traveling, dogs, food, classic movies, anime, mountain and ocean views, plants, and nature.

Check out her work, leave a review, share your thoughts with your friends and family, and be a part of a movement: helping people learn and grow through means of self-education (books).

Complete the Steps To Get Free eBooks:

Step 1: Go to amazon.com/author/destinyharris

Step 2: Filter books by "Price: Low to High"

Step 3: Download available free books

Connect W/ Destiny S. Harris

Please reach out and stay in touch. Destiny S. Harris enjoys chatting with readers.

Start a conversation today @ destinyh.com

Free Gifts!

Access courses, books, blogs, and articles at the link below:

destinyh.com

destinyharris.medium.com

destinyharris.substack.com

My Recommended Finance Books

1. Prosperity Affirmations

Speak and shift your thinking to attract wealth, abundance, and success.

2. Ladies, Get Your Financial Sh*t Together

Females traditionally fall behind men on the economic knowledge scale. Shift the pattern and get your financial sh*t together by taking the bull by the horn.

3. Stop Seeking Sugar Daddies: Be A Bad*ss Financially Independent B*tch (Financially Independent Woman)

Financial independence is one of your most powerful weapons as a female. When you're financially independent, you have options. Options are invaluable. Never take your financial independence for granted.

4. The Law Of Attraction: Create Your Life

You are the creator of your life. Look around you. What have you created? If you don't like it, learn how to shift your outer world with this book.

...

...

...